JESUS! T

Cinda,
May you find words
of encouragement within
these pages,
Love,
Pamela
Adams

Pamela Adams

DLP PUBLISHING
SWAINSBORO, GA 30401

Jesus! These Kids!

ISBN 978-1-947574-09-0

Paperback edition published 2019

Printed in the United States of America

Bulk orders are available at discounted rate.

CONTENTS

Acknowledgements

First, I would like to thank God for not giving up on me. All glory and honor go to Him. I never would have even embarked on this journey without the leading of Holy Spirit. I have saddened His heart many times with choices I made. However, He was always there waiting for me to return. I am the prodigal daughter. I thank God for allowing me to return home to Him. Truly, He is married to the backslider. His love has never failed me. I am on the path to do whatever He leads me to do. Have Thine way in me.

To my children (Jeremiah, Genesis, and Justus), I would like to say "Thank you" for the opportunity to learn as I aim to raise you to be servants of God. We do not always see eye-to-eye, but know that Mommy loves you so much. It is because of you that I continue to push. Even with tears in my eyes, you are the reasons I cannot give up. Through it all, I know I am giving you my best. I want nothing but the best for you. You can do anything with God's guidance. Never forsaken your relationship with Him.

To my Corner Sisters, thank you is not big enough. It is because of you and your encouragement that I was able to move forward with this book. Your love gave me the strength and momentum needed to just take a LEAP of faith! I will SOAR as I am being radically obedient! I am so open to all that God has for me. You all mean more than you will ever know. You know who you are!

To God's Holy Tabernacle, thank you for allowing me to be myself as I learn more and more about God. I am forever grateful to Pastor Amos Handsom, Jr. and first lady Annie Mae Handsom. You are my spiritual parents and I love you so much. Thank you for pouring out to us every time the doors of the church are open. You are inspirational. I pray I grow up to have the energy you have!

To my family, thank you for your love and support. I love you all and do not take you for granted.

To those who have touched my life from childhood until now, thank you. You know who you are. Thank you for believing in me. Thank you for your prayers. Thank you for not giving up on me. Love you.

To my mother, Dora L. Richards, you have received your wings now. You always believed in me. You always let me know that I was strong enough to handle anything life brought me. You were truly always there for me when I needed you.

I told you that I would make you proud. I know that you are smiling down from heaven. I can hear you saying, "Go, Pammie, go! Go, Pammie, go!!!" Thank you for loving me through everything. I would not be half the woman I am without your love, guidance, support and prayers. I miss you Mama. I will always hold you in my heart. You are my angel. I love you.

Foreword

Hi There,
My name is Kasundra Brown, preacher, speaker, author and mother of four sons who are grown, gone and don't need a loan. None of them have children, so there is no baby momma drama and no baby daddy trauma. Two have graduated from college with their bachelor's degrees; one is a married entrepreneur and the last is going into the US Navy after having served five years in the US Army National Guard. I think Pamela views me as a successful single parent and that may be why she offered me the privilege of writing this foreword to which I happily said, "Yes!"

I met Pamela Adams at a brunch hosted by When Women Heal, a Christian women's enrichment, entrepreneurial development and financial empowerment organization. Since there was no assigned seating, attendees were free to choose their table mates, so we sat together with a couple of my other friends. When Pamela told me the lengths she went through to get there, dropping off kids during a three-hour drive after getting very little sleep; I said to myself, "This is either a woman who wants to make a real change in her life or someone totally crazy." Either way, we were committed to sharing a table for the day. During our conversation she told me about her three children, her desire to provide a better life for them, knowing that GOD has something more for her and all of that being the reason for her presence at the Brunch. She met the group's founder, Tierra Destiny Reid at another event and decided that whatever this woman did she would be involved. When she heard about the brunch, she decided that no matter what she would be there. Then I said to myself, "So she's not crazy, just determined." It is said that all most people need to succeed is to meet that one person who, by their words and actions, changes the trajectory of their lives. Tierra Destiny Reid is that person for a number of women around the world and that day I discovered that Pamela has that same capacity. Through this book, she will change the trajectory of the lives of parents all over the world.

I don't know what made you choose this book. Maybe it was the picture of the woman in the throes of a mental breakdown. Maybe it was the title, everyone can use "a little more JESUS" when it comes to raising their kids. Maybe you heard a still small voice say, "This one. It's exactly what you need." No matter the reason, I promise you will find yourself on several of the pages and help for whatever stage of the journey you're at. I ran into myself the first time in Chapter 3 - Single Parenting. I felt all the "uns" that come with the territory; unappreciated, unrecognized, undervalued, etc... I can't count the number of times I made myself listen when all I wanted to do was read or sleep. The number of Friday nights I fell asleep watching the movie the kids chose because cars, guns and bombs were of no interest to me (remember, at the time, I was the mother of two all American boys). Don't even get me started on the number of hats I had to wear while they were going through junior high and high school. I remember returning to pick up my son from a birthday party only to discover that he volunteered me to drive two of the attendees home. These girls had been dropped off with no means of getting back home and my son had no issues with giving me a taxi driver's hat without asking about my plans.

I found myself again in chapter 5, The Other Parent. My children's father and I were married. I was angry with him for our divorce. I did it right. We were friends for several years before we married. We dated for a couple of years before getting engaged and I did not become pregnant with our first child until after the wedding. He was the one I hoped and planned to spend the rest of my life with. You know like the Beatles song, When I'm 64; oh well maybe you don't know. I had to come to grips with the fact that, even though I did not love him romantically anymore, he was still my sons' father and would be a part of my life for the rest of their lives. I had to admit my share in our failed marriage, allow him to parent the way he saw fit and trust GOD to take care of my precious babies when they were with him and I was not in total control. This was an adjustment for me that Pamela discusses in great detail. If you are in this phase of the journey, while reading this book, you will know that you are not alone and receive valuable instruction on how to navigate those turbulent waters.

Focus on the Family founder Dr. James Dobson calls single parenting "the toughest job in the universe" and with good reason. As single parents, we need good advice, wise counsel and encouragement. This book provides all three. Pamela's writing is straightforward and heartfelt. As she talks about her personal journey and struggles with two "baby daddies," she is trans- parent and real about the difficulty and necessity for forgiveness. Have you ever looked at Other People's Children and wondered, "Why can't mine behave like that?" or "Why doesn't my family act like that?" What are they doing right that I'm doing wrong?" Pamela's answer to the questions that may keep you awake at night is not to give you a list of do's and don'ts that will change your kids' behavior in 30 days. Instead she will encourage you to focus on the things that matter most. Your kids are just that, your kids. Do not focus on other people's kids, instead speak life over your children and declare the future you believe GOD has in store for them. As you read this book, you will discover that you are not alone and that there is someone who has your best interest at heart. HE just so happens to be the true Master of the Universe and the Creator of Every Living Thing. Pamela's ultimate desire in writing this book comes through on every page. She wants to encourage you to keep going as a mom or dad; knowing that even though you are not a perfect parent, you are the perfect parent for your child. I wish this book had been available when I was going "through." You are blessed, because it is in your hands and you have the opportunity to get the strength and insight that you will need to successfully complete the journey. Take Care and GOD Bless!!

Rev. Kasundra R. Brown

K. R. Brown Ministries

Introduction

Let me first begin by saying "I understand". I do not know if anyone has told you that lately, but I get it. The fact that you have this book at this very moment lets me know you are possibly on the verge… and no one even knows it. Or no one cares. Being a mother is hard. Being a parent is hard. If anyone says otherwise, they are lying and the truth "ain't" in them. Hard isn't even the word.

As you prepare to read, do understand I am writing from MY experience. I am not a professional psychologist, counselor, or anything like that. What I am is a single mother of three, seeking to do my Father's will. Be warned - I am being transparent. This is not something that is easy for me. There will be some things that may rub you the wrong way. However, it is my truth.

I pray that as you read (and for some, even relate), that some nugget will help in this journey called "Parenting". This walk is very far from ease in Zion. If you are not a parent, I hope you walk away with a bit more understanding and compassion for parents. And if you are a parent, I pray you give yourself permission to have some compassion for yourself.

As we take a journey into my life as a mother, I pray you take an honest look at yourself. Be open to freedom; to dreaming; to living. I want you to walk away with hope and knowing that you, my dear, are not alone.

So here goes.

THEN...

...NOW

Chapter One: Enjoy What?

Coming towards the end of the work day, all I want to do is curl up in bed. Email runs over with requests needing my attention. My boss comes to check on me one more time. That sticky note To-do list is not cooperating. I mark off one thing and it seems five more are added. Deep sigh. "It's going to be OK", I tell myself. However, my stress levels are off the charts! I have been working on an assignment for several days and it's still not reconciled! Why won't you reconcile!?! "*Dear God, help me to ease my mind. Let my children allow me to rest when I get home. Amen.*"

I prayed the prayer, but inwardly, I do not really believe the whispered plea. However, I am hoping. After signing them out from daycare for the day, I head to the car to already hear sibling arguing. "Leave me ALONE!!" one says. "You get on my nerves!!" replies another. I breathe in deeply before getting in then calmly say, "Children, we love each other. You must learn how to get along. I won't always be here; you need one another now and then. Is everyone fastened?" There are mumblings as I head home. I do not want to hear anything right now. They continue bickering. "BE QUIET!!!" I yell. "Mommy needs a few moments of silence. Mommy has a lot on her mind." Now I feel sad within because I raised my voice, but that seems to be the only way they listen sometimes. Most times. Sigh.

Now before I continue a typical day in my life, does this sound like anything you've experienced? Maybe so. Maybe not. In this moment you must realize - I went to the post office on my break praying to see a check, only to find bills. And not just any bills! One has jumped WAY up; now I have to find out why it is so much! I need to go to the grocery store. I must decide which bill won't be paid in full and how to juggle the dates I pay them. Truth be told, I do not make enough to cover all expenses. And there is no one to go to. It is very challenging financially when you are a single parent and being thus, have accumulated debt over the years simply trying to survive. I must acknowledge, however, that if the debt was not there, I could breathe a bit easier and life would not be so hard. But smile; let's get back to a typical day.

I am home and all I still hear are petty disputes. Fussing over who does what. There is some name calling in there too. My head is throbbing. I am trying to be calm. I do not want to yell. I simply go to my bedroom, close the door, and lock it. Inside I lie on my bed and tears begin to roll. JESUS! THESE KIDS!!! I think of how life would be if I weren't a mother. I think of how my home would stay in order. Believe it or not, I ***LOVE*** for things to be in place. However, if you visit, you may not always recognize that. In fact, you may find that Hurricane Children has it in disarray. You may find a pile of clean clothes on the kitchen table. You just may find papers everywhere. Unopened mail could be spread around. Dishes may very well be in the sink. Oh, and there is DEFINITELY a pile of dirty laundry needing attention. Not to mention that the bed is not made…in any room. LOL. How do you like that!? You cannot be OCD at my place. Hmmm, come to think of it, maybe I need an OCD friend to stop by and lend a helping hand. But, back to this day.

I am crying in my room, but I cannot stay like this. I have three who need me. I must make sure they are fed and that the house is still standing. See, I used to "try" to work all day and come home and clean everything only to find that in 30 minutes or less, it looked like I did nothing. So now, as long as I've made sure they are fed, clean, and alive, I'm good. I know, I know, I KNOW. This sounds horrible. Do not judge me. I am tired mentally, emotionally and physically in *every* way. I just want some peace. Some quiet would be nice every now and then. But even shut away in my room, I don't have it. You see, there is this amazing little boy having a fit in the hall because he wants his mother's attention. And I must give him the hugs and love he deserves. To be honest, I just cannot take all of the screaming he is doing, so I let him in.

Opening the door, I hug him. Here comes my daughter. She says, "Mommy, you act like you don't want to spend time with your children." This is one of her frequent lines. Deep breath. I explain that I love my children and I just need some rest. She does not under-stand. Not really. Maybe she's not supposed to. She is nine. They do not understand how mommy is constantly giving at work, at church, at home and needs time to myself. She does not understand what it takes to run this house. She does not have to worry about anything. She shouldn't have to worry at all. None of them should.

As I am navigating the arguments, reaffirming who they are, kissing the bruises, preparing meals, figuring out how to get needs met, I ask myself questions. Why does it seem like other parents *actually* ***enjoy*** their child(ren) and I'm like "Enjoy what?" The arguments? Temper tantrums? Attitudes? Messy house? Laziness? Dirty car? Mommy, mommy, mommy? Ungratefulness? Never having any alone time? Expenses? The feeling of losing my natural born mind!? You know, the constant uneasiness within? Sometimes I'm like, "What is there to enjoy?"

By now, you may be wondering if I enjoy my children at all. Of course, I do! I love those three with all that is within me. They are the reasons I cannot and will not quit! Let me introduce you to them.

The firstborn, Jeremiah, is eleven. He is most like his mother. He is a very caring and intelligent young man. He is also a comedian and not ashamed of being himself. Do not be surprised to see him doing a silly dance, totally comfortable in the skin he's in. I will never forget one day when he was around four, I was getting on him in the car. Out of the blue, he said, "Easy tiger". I could do nothing but laugh out loud, literally! The things children say!

During my depressed days carrying him, there were times I wondered if I should keep him. I felt that way because of how I was being treated and ostracized by, it seems, everyone. I felt very alone. Nonetheless, I pushed through all that and carried my son. Jeremiah is a very special young man. Before he was born, I wound up spotting, and went to the hospital. Turns out the umbilical cord was wrapped around his neck and an emergency c-section was performed. I say that the enemy wanted to take him out before he was born because of his destiny. I have witnessed my son experiencing the Presence of God. He knows God is real. When he was one, he told me I was pregnant. I will never forget that night. My sister-in-law and I were watching television while he played with blocks. He came to me three times and lifted my gown. Each time he went back to his blocks. I then asked, "Jeremiah, what are you looking for?" He said, "Girl."

That was the first time he had EVER said that word. Fast forward to the next month, I found out I was pregnant. Later, I found out it was indeed a girl! I call him my little prophet.

Genesis is nine. She is very much a girlie-girl and full of energy! She has a smile that will brighten any room! She is a ball of fire and does not mind sharing what she's thinking. She loves to dance and laugh! She is sensitive and does not like seeing me cry. She is like her mother; she can laugh until she cries. When her funny bone is tickled, there is no telling when she will be able to calm down.

My daughter is a challenge. She is very much a daddy's girl. That is sometimes a bit frustrating. She tends to think that when I say something she does not like, that she can just go to daddy and all will be as she wants. Her dad and I do work together to assure her that we are on the same page, and that she must obey and be respectful. She can get a major attitude. And I majorly want to take her back to when I was a girl. My mother did not play. If I even mumbled something under my breath, I thought I had lost my teeth from the blow. It did not take many of those for me to learn to keep my mouth closed. But although she is the most challenging, there is nothing I would not do for her. She loves to be around me, sometimes. LOL. And I enjoy and appreciate her boldness. I ask God to help me show her how to direct that energy and use it positively for the kingdom of God.

My baby boy is four. His name is Justus. He is another energizer bunny. He loves running around and bothering his sibling's things. This is the cause of many battles in my home. I let the older two know that he is still learning. His little smile will melt your heart! And those adorable little eyes! He has a way of wanting to fall out (a.k.a. temper tantrum) when he cannot have his way. I am working on that. Justus is also a helpful little man. He opens doors for his mommy already. He will pick up things off the floor quicker than the others sometimes. He has a thing for ears. I do not know when that will go away. So, if you see him, and he starts rubbing your ears, please do not be offended. I think it's his security blanket. He means no harm. Not to mention, this little man will pray for his mother. This makes my heart glad! He praises God in church! He is not shy one bit about singing and giving God the glory and honor!

I really do love my children. There are so many moments of laughter and love that we've shared. I do not take for granted those moments where we all may just be watching a movie…and there are no arguments, just laughing. My children aren't always fussing. They do love each other. It brings me great joy to watch my oldest showing the youngest how to do things. He is protective of his baby brother. I love it when I see all them loving on each other. Giving hugs. Crying because the other is hurt. I know they love each other although it is not always evident.

I look forward to enjoying more time with them. I want to be able to take them places and show them things I did not get to experience growing up. I want them to know that there is more to life than what they currently see every day. I want them to be able to see other cultures. I desire for them to know what they do and don't like because they have had the exposure. I do not want them limited to Swainsboro. I took them to see Disney on Ice and my daughter commented about all the ice skaters being one race. I took that moment to point out there was another lady of a different race skating too. I let her know that, regardless of color, anyone can do or be anything they want. I let her know that if that is something she wants to do, she can! I want them to know they can do anything they desire so long as it brings glory to God.

Chapter Two: Other People's Children

Have you ever wondered, "Why can't my children act like other people's children?" I have been in places and seen children around the same ages as mine sitting down. They are so well mannered. I do not witness any tantrums. The siblings are actually getting along. And the children are listening to the parent(s)…THE FIRST TIME! Oh, my Lord!!!

Or have you gone to visit someone who has children and the house is spotless? Like, '*How* do you do that?' How is it their house looks clean, while mine currently looks like a tornado, hurricane and tsunami came to visit?

Life is hard enough without adding on the weight of comparing yourself (or your children) to others. Honestly, I do not know what goes on with that family behind closed doors. I do not know how those children act anywhere else. This moment could have been an answered prayer for the parent(s) involved. But because I saw them at one moment, I begin to feel like I am less than. I have frequently stated and felt like I was failing as a mother. Why? They do not listen. They just don't. It seems as though all of the talking isn't going anywhere. Sometimes it feels like my prayers are for what? I do not see change. In fact, I think that attitude just went to another level.

Why is it we feel that other people always have things better? It appears that the grass is greener on their side. We scroll through social media seeing pictures of happy families. Husbands with wives…smiling. Mothers, fathers, and children appearing to love, appreciate, and delight in each other. I wonder, "Why?" Why didn't my marriage work? Why do I have two 'baby daddies'? Why aren't my children as well behaved as theirs? Why didn't my family act like that? Why am I having to do life alone? Why don't I have people in my life to lend a helping hand? Why? Why? Why?

God is looking at us and saying, "Why NOT you?" You see, there are times we face things not for ourselves, but for someone else. Why would God do that to us? Because He's God. God knows you are strong enough to handle the situation. He knows He can trust you to not give up, to not quit. Our heavenly Father sees the big picture. We don't. We see in part. We must trust that the road we are on is where we are meant to be. We have an expected end.

Now, you may be saying, "But I deviated from the path God had for me. I made choices that took me down paths I could have avoided. You don't know what I've done. You don't know all the tears I've shed because of this or because of that." Well, let me be the first to say that I understand. I knew God wanted great things for me. Yet, I made decisions that went against what I knew to be right. I strayed away. And because I did so, I shed many tears. I went through many avoidable events. However, I am also here to let you know about the grace and mercy of God! Even when I did wrong, He was there waiting on me. I had people praying for me. My mother, God rest her soul, put me in the hands of God. I know her prayers helped give me the strength to pull, to fight, to keep going. I know for myself: God is married to the back-slider. I know for myself that although I did not always make the best choices, God STILL has a plan! I took the longer route, but I made it! I am not allowing my past to bind me. I will be all He has called me to be. Why?

Because I have decided to trust Him; I have decid-ed to follow Jesus.

Stop looking at "other people's children" and focus on the ones you have. I do not know fully *who* I am raising up, but I speak life! I am raising up young men of valor! I am raising a young lady who will be a woman on fire for God! I decree that my children will walk in the ordinances of God! I have kingdom children! Sometimes it does not look like it. Sometimes it does not feel like it. But that is where your FAITH comes in!

Hebrews 11:1 KJV says, "Now faith is the substance of things hoped for, the evidence of things not seen." The NLT version says it this way— "Faith is the confidence that what we hope for will actually happen; it gives us assurance about things we cannot see." Where is your faith!? I won't look at other people's children. Instead, I will continue to focus on the three He has entrusted to me. Does this journey get hard? You bet your bottom dol-lar it does. But I know a man from Galilee who died and rose just for me! Just for my children! Just for you and yours! It is time to get out of your pity party and allow that faith to rise like a sweet perfume!

If you go a little further in Hebrews 11, verse six says, "But without faith it is impossible to please him: for he that cometh to God must **believe** that he is, and that he is a rewarder of them that diligently seek him." God is looking for action. Are you seeking Him on behalf of yourself and your children? Faith works when you use it! James 2:17 NIV states that "faith, by itself, if it is not accompanied by action, is dead." We must learn to act on it. You often hear that actions speak louder than words. It is time for you to speak life over your children and act as if it is already done! Our words are a creative force! We have exactly what we say. If you continue speaking down to that child, guess what? They will continue being what you are calling them until they start speaking life over themselves. But when you begin speaking the promises of God over them! My God! Change is coming! So, I do not care what it looks like, you keep speaking! You keep praying! You keep praising! You keep instilling the righteousness of God in your children! Decree and declare that they are who GOD says they are! Parent speak life and do your part to raise them to be champions for Christ. You do your best and allow God to do the rest.

"Train up a child in the way he ***should*** go: and when he is old, he will not depart from it."[1]

[1] Proverbs 22:6 KJV

Chapter Three: Single Parenting

Being a single mother can truly be one of the most difficult things life can bring. Looking back to adolescence, this is *so* not how I saw my life. This is not how things were supposed to be. I was supposed to be married to a wonderful husband 'til death did us part. My children were not to arrive on the scene until after the wedding day. Before they arrived, I was supposed to have traveled to places I had never been. I was supposed to have experienced life with the love of my life and be "ready" to become a mother. That was my dream.

That is NOT how my life turned out. I got pregnant before I was married. I suffered depression during that time. I felt like I had no one. I disappointed my mother, my church and myself. I felt that I had let God down. Mama did the best she could in letting me know I should wait. She told me on numerous occasions that it was not worth it. It is no fault of hers that my life turned out how it has. I was taught what was right and wrong. I grew up in church. We never lacked what we needed. Growing up, I watched my mother raise my sister and I without a husband. He died when I was in kindergarten. She made it look effortless. My mother always made sure we had food, clothing and a roof over our heads. We weren't dressed in name brands, but we had all of our needs met. After becoming a mother myself, I often apologized to her for being "active" and into everything. She would always laugh and tell me, "Pam, if I made it, you will too. You're strong."

Strong. I *hate* having to be strong all the time. To be strong is to be "able to withstand great force or pressure." [2] Occasionally, those deemed "strong" need someone too. From the outside looking in, we often see a person taking care of things like a boss. What you do not see is that within, they are dying. Within, they are barely keeping their head above water. Within, they are screaming for help. Within, they are crying rivers and oceans. People need to understand that just because one can take care of things alone, does not mean everything is ok. It does not mean that at all. What it does mean is we do what we have to do in order to survive. I do what I must for my children because they did not ask to be here. It was my

---

[2] Google search engine

decisions that got them here. Being a single parent is NOT what I desired, however, it is my current reality. I refuse to not try to do my best to raise these three amazing, yet challenging, children I have been given.

Single parents don't always get the recognition due them. Every person that has a child is NOT a parent. To parent means to be present in the lives of your children. To parent means providing the needs of those children. To parent means to know what your children like, dislike, what their behavior is like, etc. Being a parent is more than having a child. You have to give up your wants for theirs.

You do not always get to do what you want. I have seen parents who always put their kids off on the grand-parents so they can go out and do whatever it is they want. That is not fair to your parents or those children. Some "parents" put their kids off on anyone who will keep them. They are always looking for a way out. No. A parent is there. A parent takes their children with them. Do not get me wrong; I wish I could have a bit more time to myself. I do not always take them with me. For exam-ple, I do not always take them to the grocery store because they ask for things that are not on my list. They start having attitudes because I say “No, mommy can’t get that.” They want to cry and act out, drawing unwanted attention to me and my obvious ability NOT to be able to control them. That is not what I am referring to here. I mean there are literally grandparents and others raising the children you were given. And it is not ok to dump them off on everybody else. They are your responsibility, but we will talk more on that later.

Parents are expected to be and do so much. I am expected to be mommy, doctor, nurse, cook, maid, uber, hair stylist, mentor, coach, teacher, expert of all subjects, encourager, happy at all times, and the list goes on and on. Well, I am not happy all the time. In fact, most days I am tired. When people ask me how I am doing, most of the time you will hear “I am tired”. My mind seems to never want to stop working. Even while lying down I am constantly thinking. “Do the kids have enough clean clothes for the week? How am I going to pay this bill? Should I call this one and let them know that I really don’t have enough to pay them? Or do I write the check praying that other bills don’t clear at the same time? Why do all the socks disappear? Where do I look to complete this work assignment? God, youth service is Tuesday and I still haven't heard from You on what to talk about." Just continuous, uninterrupted thoughts. So even if I lie down, it's more than likely that I am still tired because my mind has not rested.

What I am learning to do is give myself a break. This is kind of hard when I want everything to be 'perfect'. I am learning to grant myself grace and a little mercy. It is easy sometimes to grant those things to others, but what about yourself? Grace is "extending kindness to the unworthy."[3] Mercy deals with "compassion or forgiveness shown toward someone whom it is within one's power to punish or harm."[2]

Oftentimes we punish ourselves by replaying what we did or did not do in situations. We rerun how things should have, could have, or would have been. I know there were many times I would replay how things would be different if I had made a different choice. However, I know I cannot change anything in my past. The only

---

[3] Caroline Austin – *https://www.quora.com/What-is-the-difference-between-grace-and-mercy-in-Christianity*

thing I can do is learn from past choices and work toward making better ones now and in the future. How about showing yourself a bit of kindness for still standing? How about giving yourself a little compassion for making choices out of a broken place? Just as our Father gives grace and mercy to us, we must give it to ourselves.

Parenting is not an easy job, but you can make it through. It all has to do with healing and reprogramming your mind to align with Christ's thoughts for you. The Bible is full of promises for us. It is our job to open the book and allow those words to wash over our dirty, tired, and weary souls. Allowing Christ to cleanse us from within begins with forgiving others…and forgiving yourself.

Chapter Four: What's Going on Within?

Are you holding on to your past? Have you truly forgiven yourself? If not, it is time to let go. You cannot move into what God has for you holding on to bad decisions. God has so much in store for you. He wants to use you for His glory. There is nothing you have done so wrong that He won't forgive you. He has been waiting to renew, restore, and realign your steps. He knows the plans He has for you. They are plans to prosper you and give you an expected end (Jeremiah 29:11). But you cannot get it if you choose to stay stuck in the past.

Have you noticed that you are not where you want to be in life? Do you feel it is partly because of your children? Have you taken the time to look within yourself? Does it feel like you are taking one step forward, only to be knocked back six? Are you always thinking negatively and blaming it on your children? Did you really want to be a parent? Do you feel stuck? Do your children make you feel like you're trapped? If you have answered "yes" to any of these, it may be time for you to pause and reflect. Often the answers are within as to why we feel how we do and why we respond the way that we do.

We must understand that our actions have consequences. If you play with fire, you are going to be burned eventually. My mother would talk to me about the men I chose to talk to. She would let me know her honest opinion and I would respond, "No mom, he's not going to do those things to me." Sometimes love (or rather, lust) is so blind. I was warned about what would and could be the outcome. God loved me enough to send the warning, but because of the vessel being my mother, I did not want to listen.

My mother was very strict on me growing up. I was not allowed to do anything. I could not go to a friend's house or even be active in school clubs. She just didn't believe in allowing us to do anything. In fact, my first time joining a school club and fully participating happened my senior year of high school…second semester. I joined FBLA and thoroughly enjoyed it. Looking back though, I now realize that she just did not want me to be exposed to the bad in the world. In her own way, she felt she was protecting me.

When I graduated from college with my Associate degree, I went on to get my bachelor's degree away from home. It was then I decided to become 'grown' and experience things for myself. I never was the clubbing type, but I did make a choice to give up my virginity. In doing so, I later became pregnant at 21, having my first son at 22. We later got married; I thought I would live my fairy tale. It did not happen the way I thought, and years later, we divorced.

There was a time I blamed my mother for not allowing me to experience life while in her home. I became distant because I did not want to hear what she had to say concerning my decisions. I would not be blatantly disrespectful. I just decided not to talk or come around as much. As things crumbled in my marriage, I shared some things with her, but we did not have the close relationship we had when I lived with her. This hurt her, but I felt I was protecting myself. She just did not understand.

In March 2018, my mother died. What I am glad and proud to say is that before she did, our relationship was healed. We indeed had that mother-daughter bond again. It took me a while to let go. There were tears and prayers to God to help me release all the times I didn't get to do this or that. I prayed for the strength to forgive her. In hindsight, I realize my mother did the best she could. She was not perfect, but she was who God wanted to raise me. My mother went through bad relationships and only wanted better for me. Everything my mother told me concerning my relationships came to pass. I just did not want to listen. It is not her fault that I made poor choices despite having been warned.

I had to take responsibility for my actions. My marriage did not work out. I thought I would marry the second baby daddy. That didn't happen. My life is not where I thought it would be. However, I decided that despite every past decision, I will move forward. My past decisions cannot be changed, but I can still be the woman God created me to be. I will be who He predestined me to be!

It is time to let go. It is time to stop blaming everyone else for your current situation. It is time to forgive. Sometimes we "say" we have forgiven someone, but when just the name is mentioned, we feel "some-type-of-way". If you cannot talk about what happened without anger or rage, you have not forgiven them. If just the thought of that person makes you cringe, you have not forgiven them. If every time you see them, you want to run the other way, you have not forgiven them. If the only thoughts you have are for their demise, you have definitely not forgiven them. It is time to forgive the people who hurt you. It is time to forgive those who did not *and* could not see your worth.

It is time to forgive yourself. Forgive the broken you who made the "not-so-wise" decisions. It is time to free yourself. You must be free. Lay aside every weight that so easily besets you because baby, it's time for you to fly! It is time to work on what's going on within. For some, going to the altar may be enough. Then there are others who need to seek counseling. There is nothing wrong with that. Sometimes it takes having a person who does not know you, to help you see some truths and in taking steps to become better.

Whatever avenue you must take, whatever you need to do to free yourself, it is time to do so. Once you have, I know that God's peace that passes all understanding will

wash over you. It is time to really see what's going on within and deal with it so that you can win!

Chapter Five: The Other Parent

Now this chapter could easily be about placing blame. Who did what and who hurt who. I could certainly talk about the many emotional rollercoasters encountered before each child was even thought of. However, #WhenWomenHeal, we use our power to the benefit of everyone. To talk against the men who are my children's fathers would show how little character I have. And that is not me. This chapter is written to encourage you to think outside yourself. I understand there were issues. I understand there is a reason you may not be with the person(s) who helped to create your child(ren). However, those reasons should not allow you to keep your children away from that parent unless there truly is danger. Let's look at my situation in hopes that you can inwardly reflect on yours.

I have two very different men who are fathers to my children. When I tell you they are like night and day…that is an understatement. I found myself with each person during different places in my life, both of which were not all that healthy. With the first, I was not really experienced in having a relationship. My mother did not allow me that privilege in her home. In fact, I was scared to death of trying her. Maybe that is not your experience with your parent(s), but Mama Dora wasn't the one I wanted to play with. In the second relationship, I was very broken. I would say going through a failed marriage broke me in a way I never want to experience again.

In both, I was very naïve. I set out to ONLY see the good in a person. A wise woman, known as Dr. Maya Angelou, said, "When someone shows you who they are, believe them the FIRST time." My God how things would have been so different if these words had been my motto. However, they were not, and I cannot change any decision made with past relationships.

They say looking back is 20/20. Oh, how looking back can show you things you miss because of the desire to just have someone in your life. You will take and accept almost anything just to NOT be alone. Chile, please. I am so beyond that now! Glory to the Most High God! However, getting to this place has been a process. I used to need validation from others. I wanted to know I meant something, that I was special because "they" said so.

Having others to confirm and approve who I am puts too much power in their hands. I no longer need this. I KNOW God created me special. I am "fearfully and wonderfully made."[4] The only thing that matters is what my Father thinks of me. My worth is found in Him! My identity is found in Christ alone. I do not need a man to tell me who I am because I am discovering who I am each day. I am on a journey to wholeness. I am on a journey of healing. To heal, you must forgive.

There was a time I hated the men who are my children's fathers. They could have dropped from the face of the earth and I would have been fine with that. This honesty is not pretty. I am not proud to say those words, but it is the truth.

In my hurt, I hated them. I could see nothing but what had been done to me. I could only replay the tears. I could only see how much I GAVE. When I didn't have it to give, I gave from my empty place. How do you give from a broken vessel? But I did. I loved as much as I could from an unfilled heart. I poured what I had into

---

[4] Psalm 139:14

each relationship. Giving my body was the ultimate way I showed them how much they meant. This was never forced. I did it willingly. I knew that was not God's way, but to keep them, I felt I had to. That was the ultimate sacrifice. And children were birthed from it.

In my hurt, I put up walls to try to protect my children. At least that's what I told myself. You see, there were things I did not agree with. Since I did not agree, I would not allow the children to spend time with their fathers. I eventually allowed interaction with the first father. It has taken longer with the second father, but it is happening. Why? Because it is important for my children to know who their dads are. It is important they know who their families are.

Truth is, I was thinking more of my feelings than my children's feelings. I was hurt, not them. I had to ask God many times to help me to remove these intense feelings of hatred. I cried so many times because of the bitterness that had begun to form in my heart towards these men. I knew I could not allow bitterness to take root. And if it had, only Jesus could pull it up.

I went to the throne of grace so many times. I am not going to tell you that forgiving is easy. It was not a one-time deal with me. Sometimes you 'think' you have forgiven someone until you see them, or someone mentions their name and then, your whole atmosphere changes. That happened countless times. I thought I was good… until. But what I can tell you is that if you are sincere in letting that mess go, God will heal the brokenness. He did just that for me. He broke the chains of unforgiveness. He demolished the shackles of self-pity. He has given me a new start because I was willing to let go.

I apologized for my actions in the relationships. I asked forgiveness because everything I did was not always right either. #WhenWomenHeal, we are willing to see both sides of the story. I know I was not always right. My attitude was not always right. And when pushed, my mouth was not always right either. But I am thankful for reflection. I am grateful to be able to truly look back and say I learned from my actions. There were some hard lessons that very well could have been avoided. But without them, I could not share my story. I could not tell you I know God is a deliverer. I would not be able to testify that I am still here with my mind intact had I not gone through. I didn't know my own strength.

I could not write this chapter and have you think that everything about those men is all bad. Everyone has good qualities. I give God praise that I can get a Saturday to myself every now and again. I need a break! It is hard raising children and I had to admit I needed a break...even if all I did was sleep.

I had to ask God to heal every broken, hidden thing within me. My dear friend, Michelle Flagg, said something that hit me to my core. She said, "I had to learn how to be *a* parent and not *the* parent." She was talking about herself, but those words stuck with me. I could look at my life as a mother and see how I was acting like I was the only parent. I had to take a deep sigh and really go to God. When you ask to see yourself, He will show you yourself. The question is, are you willing to take steps to change for the best once He shows you?

I was hurting in that area but did not want to admit it. After crying out to God, I decided I would no longer be in the way. This was a much-needed step for me to take. I would no longer allow feelings of hurt, anger, frustration, and bitterness to get in the way of my children having a relationship with their fathers. Again, I had been hurt, not the children. I put pride aside and asked for forgiveness. I am on a healing journey. I truly only want the best for my children and I pray blessings over their fathers and their families. Life is too short to keep mess in your heart.

Co-parenting is what you make of it. I know there can be peace after the storm *if* all parties are willing to work together for the child's sake. There must be mutual respect. Let your child(ren) see you cooperating, with love for them being the center. There should not be any disrespect at all. Our children can see and feel what their parents radiate emotionally. They are not ignorant. The only thing they should feel and know is, "*My parents love me*". My parents support me. My parents can get along without drama, attitudes, and arguments. This is not always *easy*. But it is possible.

And if for some reason you cannot reach that harmonious space after trying, leave it be. Period. Protect your peace. Protect it by any means necessary. If you have done all you know to and there is still drama, you must do what is best for you and your children.

Regardless of anything, your child needs you to be in the best space possible. You must be in your right mind. No matter what, mama, your child needs you. And they need you to be able to make clear decisions raising them. You cannot do that with your mind clouded by unnecessary situations. You cannot do that emotionally unstable. You must continue in becoming the best version of yourself. Your children need you. They need the BEST you can offer.

In looking back, and knowing it is God's design that we marry before intercourse, I know I started off wrong. You cannot do things your way and expect God to bless your mess. He is not required to do that. He watches after His word to perform it. Not our words. Not our actions. But even in my mess, He extended grace. He extended mercy. God was always there waiting for my return. And if Christ is the example I am living by, who am I to not extend mercy as well? Our children need both of their parents, *when possible*. It is our job to let go of pride and allow the other parent to be that in their child(ren)'s lives.

Chapter Six: The Enemy's Lies

Did you know that you have an enemy? He is the father of lies. Some may even say he is the great deceiver. "He was a murderer from the beginning. He has always hated the truth, because there is no truth in him. When he lies, it is consistent with his character; for he is a liar and the father of lies."[5]

The devil, satan, lucifer (or any other name you know him by) is your enemy. He seeks to "steal, kill, and destroy"[6] you. One of the main ways he does this is to give you suggestions that are against God's word. These suggestions are nothing more than lies.

Your adversary, the devil, studies you. He wants to be able to appeal to your fleshly desires. He examines your behavior so that he can present the things you want. If you are lonely, he's not going to send just anyone your way. He will send what looks good to you. It is going to be oh, so shiny. It will sparkle as dear gold. But friend be careful to "believe not every spirit, but try the spirits

---

[5] John 8:44 NLT
[6] Reference to John 10:10

whether they are of God."[7] Everything that glitters definitely isn't gold.

A lie is "a false statement made with deliberate intent to deceive; an intentional untruth; a falsehood."[8] The devil is not named the father of lies for nothing. He is committed to misleading as many people as he can. Hell was created for him and the fallen angels, but misery loves company.

Satan wants to misinform you about who you truly are. He will twist words and play mental games with you…if you let him. He wants you to feel like a failure so much until you do not even want to live. You will be ready to take your own life. That is a trick because to die without accepting Christ is to die and go straight to hell.

Listening to the ideas your enemy plants will have you feeling as if nothing you do is good enough. You will feel that you are not a good parent. He will have you insecure in how you look. He taunts you. "You are just like your daddy (mama). No one loves you. God certainly doesn't. You've done too much wrong for Him to love

---

[7] I John 4:1 KJV
[8] Dictionary.com

you. WHO would love a thing like you? God won't forgive you for that, you know. He has left you alone to raise these kids. No one supports you. Just shut up and forget ever telling anyone about your struggles. You must hide in your past. Don't open up about those childhood nightmares. What was done in that house must remain in that house. Oh, and remember when you did that? Yep. God let that happen to you. Just keep living any ole way. You don't have to be moral. And church? Chile, it don't take all that. Nobody has time to be running to no church every day of the week. Continue having sex without being married. Continue making all these babies that will live in single parent homes. That's how you do it! You're never going to be enough you ugly, unpleasant, nasty little thing you. Keep being petty!!! That's right. Run everybody away with your disagreeable attitude. I ***love*** that foul language! Tell him again how he ain't nothing! Girl, you are on a roll today! Give them all those pieces of your mind. Don't hold nothing back!"

That is just a little of the deception the devil speaks to your mind. It is truly a battle going on within us. Our words have power and your thoughts are words. If he can get you to thinking about all the negative things that has happened to you, he will try to use that to keep you bound. But let me share a few truths with you.

You are enough. You are "fearfully and wonderfully made"[9] in the image of God. You have the face, body, hair, voice, and mind that God created just for you. Even if you look just like your parents, you are unique! Own it! Love being who you are!

There is NO ONE else who can do what you do and how you do it. You were created for greatness! It is time to dream again. Dream big! I mean dreams so enormous, it requires faith greater than the size of a mustard seed. The desires in your heart are not there for nothing. They are there for you to do it! It is time to KNOW you CAN do it! Start the business. Write the book. Go after the desires placed within your heart. Nothing is impossible when you allow Jesus to lead and guide you! Ask Him to order your steps in His word. Seek His plans for your life. They are GREATER than your wildest imaginations. You

---

[9] Psalm 139:14

have no clue how much He is waiting to bless your socks off! Just trust Him and walk in obedience.

You have what it takes to raise your children. No one else can raise them, love them and encourage them like you can. You will NOT lose your mind! You will NOT throw in the towel. Yes, being a mother is hard. But you, my dear, aren't a quitter. You are more than a conqueror! The Greater One lives on the inside of you. You CAN do ALL things through Christ's strength. You are stronger than you ever thought possible. Fight the good fight of faith! You have what your children need. Even when you don't know how ends will be met, trust God. He has a plan. Never are the righteous forsaken! Your children will have ALL they need.

Nothing you have ever done will stop God's love for you. He is married to the backslider. There is no thing that catches Him by surprise. Nothing. He is waiting for you to come back home! He is standing with arms wide open longing to wash away the sin, the pain, the shame, the hurt, the guilt. He is waiting for you to lay aside the weights, to come to the altar, to repent and start over. Release all the heaviness you have been carrying. You were not built for this battle. It is time to give it to the Lord. God is waiting for you. He is right where you left Him. Or He is waiting to be found by you. Call to Him earnestly and be set free!

You do not have to be stuck in your past decisions! Embrace the daily new mercies you are given. Forgive yourself. You did the best you could in the state you were in. Grant yourself a little mercy. Let go of the past because it is time to soar! It is time to walk and not be weary. Do not remain comfortable in your cocoon. You are changing into a beautiful butterfly, despite how ugly the past seemed. It is time to spread your wings and prepare to fly! Your time is NOW!

Chapter Seven: Responsibility as a Mother

Whether you planned for the child(ren) you have, or it just happened, you have a major responsibility. Period. There is no getting around this fact. It does not matter the circumstance that led to your being a parent. The child is here and needs you. They need the BEST you.

Right now you may be struggling. Struggling to pay the bills. Struggling to put food on the table. Struggling to get out of bed in the morning because depression is weighing you down. Struggling to keep your mind toget-her. I understand it is no easy task raising these growing individuals…and trying to raise them to be productive, kind, and respectful children. My God! It's so hard! But it is what we must do.

The children you have are in your custody for a reason. There is a purpose and a plan for your life and theirs. And, no, that plan is not to drive you to the "looney bin" aka the "crazy house". No. It is bigger than that! The enemy wants us to focus so much on the neg-ative aspects, we lose sight of the bigger picture. God had a specific objective in mind when he created all of us. Our lives are to bring Him glory.

As a mother, I am responsible for the wellbeing of my children. I must be sure that they are fed, clothed, sheltered, educated, and safe. I am to do my best to make sure they are not around any and everybody. There are many wolves in disguise these days. I must discern who I can allow my children to be around. But above all of this, I believe, I must show my children they are loved.

I tell them daily how much I love them. I often add on that I do not know how long my life will be and I never want them to forget that I love them. But it is not enough to only say it. When they come to me and want to talk, I must make time and space for them. There have been so many times where I was doing something else and did not listen. Like *truly* hear their heart. I told them they could talk to me, but when they came, I was too busy. I am learning to stop and be intentional in listening to them. This is a definite "work-in-progress". However, if I do not do it now, they definitely will not talk to me later. I want an open line of communication with them because I know what it feels like to not be able to open up to those closest to me.

It is my responsibility to nurture them. I must be sure to help them develop into what God has created them to be. I must pay attention to the gifts and talents God has blessed them with. I need to hear them when they express what they do and do not like. For example, I was going to sign Jeremiah up for football. On the way to the Recreation Department, he said, "Mom, I don't want to play football. I want to play baseball." Now I could have *made* him play, but instead, I listened. I want him to give his best in anything he does. He would not have if I had forced it. We should not try to force our children to be anything but who they are. We have lived our childhood. We should not try to make them into the child we wanted to be. Allow your children to be their own, unique person.

It is my job to tell my children the truth. Many times, we sugarcoat things trying to shield them. Now, I am in no way saying our children have to know every single detail of a situation. I am saying when they come and ask you about anything, be honest. There have been many times my children did not understand why I was no longer married to their dad. I never told them anything to make them hate him. No. That is daddy and you love him. I did let them know that things do not always work out the way you want. And it is ok.

Truth does not always feel good. It can hurt like crazy, but it is needed. Do not lie to your children. There have been times my children would ask me if I was ok. I would lie and say “Yes”, but I wasn’t. I am learning to tell them (and everyone else) the truth. Yes, we will do this. No, we are not doing that. No, I don’t feel like doing this right now. Be real with them and everyone else in your life.

It is my job to teach them about life. Life is hard. I have to share the lessons I have learned from decisions I made concerning finances, relationships, education, etc. They need to know they can avoid what I fell into. They need to know their relationship with Christ is the most important relationship they should have.

They need to know you have to work for what you want. Things are not just given to adults, at least not the ones I know. LOL. I have to work. Sometimes children are so ungrateful and think you *have to* give them what they want. No, sugar. If you have a roof over your head, clothes, shoes, food to eat, and you are in a safe place, everything else is extra. Do your best as their provider. Do not beat yourself up over what you cannot do. You are doing plenty. My children don't like when I say "no", but it is a part of life. I have been told no so many times. And guess what? I'm just fine. It did not kill me. In fact, it just may have saved my life.

Children need to know that it is ok not to do everything perfectly the first time. It is ok to make a mistake. It is human. When your child is upset because they did not get it right the first time, take that opportunity to teach them about learning from the experience. Let your children know they are more than a grade or a test. I have had to deal with my son in being so disappointed in himself because he did not have the best grade on a standardized test. Grades are important, but they do not define who you are and what you know. My son is brilliant. I encourage him to continue doing his best. As long as he is doing that, I'm good.

It is my responsibility to let my children know that it is ok to ask for help. In the midst of our own extremely busy lives, we must make time to help our children. Let them know you are there to assist them.

Needing assistance is human. If you try to do everything on your own, you will lose your mind. Part of being a responsible adult is knowing when to let someone else do what you cannot. Be an example. Show your children that even you need help sometimes. Do not pretend to be some superhero that never needs anything. Doing so is only setting them up for failure and a lot of stress.

I must let my children know they should stand up for themselves and for what they believe. You are not a doormat for anyone. You do not have to take just anything. It is not ok to hurt others and you should not allow them to hurt you. If someone wants you to do something that isn't right, you do not have to do it. Let them know the value of doing the right thing.

Let your children know they are important. They do not need the approval of the "in-crowd". They are special and unique. Our children need to know that they do not have to fit in. My children have had to deal with bullying. I also had to deal with the same thing. Children tease them about how they look and act. I always encourage them to be themselves regardless. Teach your child to treat others with kindness and respect.

Show your child what self-love looks like. If you instill this in them at an early age, it will be second nature as they grow up and mature. They won't allow people to treat them any-kind-of way.

Let us help them to not go through what some of us did. Teach them about what is and is not important. Teach and show them how not to give up; to have the tenacity to complete what they start. Let us give them a better chance to succeed by teaching them through example.

Remember, none of us are perfect. You just continue being the best parent you can be. Do your very best to raise successful, respectful children. Don't give up. Even when it looks like things are not turning out ok, keep trying. Nothing is happenstance. You will get through this. We both will. We cannot stop because it gets difficult, challenging, and demanding. Always be intentional in learning how to be and do things better. Be ok with not having it all together. Know that your children may not understand all you have sacrificed right now, but one day

things will become clearer. Give your children the best you can and trust that God will do the rest!

Chapter Eight: The Prayer

Pray the following prayer with an open mind, heart, and spirit. If you are a father reading this, insert father or dad in the place of mother. Allow the Presence of God to wash over you. It's ok if you smile, cry, dance…whatever. Just be sincere.

****

Dear Heavenly Father,

I come to You as humble as I know how. Forgive me for all deeds done knowingly and unknowingly against You and Your word. Father hear my prayer.

I come to You asking You to help me keep my sanity. Being a parent is hard. It's the most grueling job I have right now, and I don't want to fail. When my heart is overwhelmed, lead me to the Rock that's higher than I. You, Jesus, are the Rock. You are the source of my being. I can do nothing without You. You are the source of my strength.

If I don't know You, come into my heart. May I learn the ways of You and teach them to my children. Let us hear Your voice and move in obedience. Make Yourself real in our lives. Let us know who You truly are and experience You like never before. Give us a ravenous hunger and thirst for righteousness and to live our lives to bring You glory.

Give me clarity, O God. Help me to see clearly the plots and plans of the enemy in my life and lives of my children. Let me see and avoid every pit satan has plotted for my demise and theirs.

Teach me how to be the mother I am supposed to be, the mother I am meant to be. Let me know and accept that it's ok to not be perfect. It's ok to not know it all. It's ok to not be ok all the time. Help me to always look to You, to seek You and Your wisdom in every area.

Let me not fall into the trap of comparison, O God. Let me focus on my life and my children. Help me to continue to do my best as a parent and know that it's good enough. I am enough. I am equipped to do this job the best way I know how. And what I don't know, Lord, show me. Teach me.

Help me to not lose sight of the big picture. Show me how to bring my thoughts AND words in alignment with the destinies You have for my children. When I want to give up, let me see them as You see them. Let me speak words of wisdom, life, and truth over them in spite of what I see.

God, help me not to take my frustrations out on my children. Let me pause and release every irritation and annoyance to You. If I have to leave to scream, to cry, to pray, I'll do it. I don't want to add things that my children will have to grow up and heal from. Help me catch myself and come to You.

Open the eyes of my heart Lord. Open the eyes of my enlightenment. Help me to forgive myself for every wrong decision made. I am no longer that person and will not be bound by the past. I will dream again. I will love again. I will move forward in power and strength that only comes from You. I am not the same. I let Your love rest, rule, and abide in me.

Cleanse every area of my heart. Wash me and I'll be white as snow. Create in me a clean heart, O God, renewing a right spirit within me. Cast me not away from Your Presence and take not Your Holy Spirit from me.

God, help me to release every broken piece of my past. Help me to truly forgive every person who has ever hurt me. And for those really heartbreaking incidents, show me how to deal with them and heal from them. Your word declares that I am more than a conqueror. I want to truly get past the past. I release it all to You now.

Give me strength to share my story to help others who are facing what I've gone through and survived. Let me be a light in the midst of darkness.

I speak peace to the minds of my children. I know that they are facing and will face things that I didn't as a child. I speak peace to the storms that they go through and don't always share. As I heal, let our relationship as parent and child heal. Let us grow and bond even the more.

Cover my children, Jesus. I cannot be with them everywhere they go. Keep them safe from all danger. Let what I've taught them rise up when it needs to. Send godly influences in their lives. Remove those who are up to no good and seek the fall of my children.

Help me to allow my children to be themselves. Stir up their gifts and reveal them to me. Show me what I need to do to add wind to the flame of their talents and natural abilities!

Lord, even when I am so tired and exhausted, let me always encourage my children to talk to me openly about all things. Give me wisdom in how to respond to what they say – even the things I may not agree with. Let them see that I respect and love them regardless. And in those moments of disagreement, show us how to respectfully and lovingly agree-to-disagree and move on in love.

God, when it comes to disciplining my children, show me how to do so in love. Discipline is a way to show that I care. You correct us because You love us. It's not because You hate us, but that You desire for us to avoid the pitfalls of life. Let me never go overboard where discipline becomes abuse. I don't want to abuse my child in any way – physically or emotionally. Give me wisdom in how to discipline my children.

Help me to do exactly what I said I would do. Don't let me tell my children one thing and don't follow up on it. They should know that what I say, I mean it, the first time.

And God, when the house is a mess, the children are all screaming, and I want to run away, help me to hide in You. Let me dwell in Your shelter and rest in Your shadow. Allow me to react in love and from a space of deep peace. I feel weak in my parenting at times, Lord, but Your strength is made PERFECT in my weakness! In those hard moments, in those moments of total and utter chaos, let me remember the truths of Your word.

I decree and declare that it is so!

In Jesus' name,

Amen and amen!

Encouragement from the Word

So let's not get tired of doing what is good. At just the right time we will reap a harvest of blessing if we don't give up. Therefore, whenever we have the opportunity, we should do good to everyone—especially to those in the family of faith.

Galatians 6:9-10 NLT

For whom the LORD loves He corrects, just as a father the son in whom he delights.

Proverbs 3:12 NKJV

Seek the Kingdom of God above all else, and live righteously, and he will give you everything you need. So don't worry about tomorrow, for tomorrow will bring its own worries. Today's trouble is enough for today.

Matthew 6:33 NLT

Don't fret or worry. Instead of worrying, pray. Let petitions and praises shape your worries into prayers, letting God know your concerns. Before you know it, a sense of God's wholeness, everything coming together for good, will come and settle you down. It's wonderful what happens when Christ displaces worry at the center of your life.

Philippians 4:6-7 MSG

Care for the [children] *that God has entrusted to you. Watch over* [them] *willingly, not grudgingly—not for what you will get out of it, but because you are eager to serve God. Don't lord it over the people assigned to your care, but lead them by your own good example.*

I Peter 5:2-3 NLT

Point your kids in the right direction—when they're old they won't be lost.

Proverbs 22:6 MSG

Parents, don't come down too hard on your children or you'll crush their spirits. Servants, do what you're told by your earthly masters. And don't just do the minimum that will get you by. Do your best. Work from the heart for your real Master, for God, confident that you'll get paid in full when you come into your inheritance. Keep in mind always that the ultimate Master you're serving is Christ. The sullen servant who does shoddy work will be held responsible. Being a follower of Jesus doesn't cover up bad work.

Colossians 3:21-25 MSG

Therefore I say to you, whatever things you ask when you pray, believe that you receive them, and you will have them.

Mark 11:24 NKJV

Folly is bound up in the heart of a child, but the rod of discipline drives it far from him.

Proverbs 22:15 ESV

Love is patient and kind. Love is not jealous or boastful or proud or rude. It does not demand its own way. It is not irritable, and it keeps no record of being wronged. It does not rejoice about injustice but rejoices whenever the truth wins out. Love never gives up, never loses faith, is always hopeful, and endures through every circumstance. Three things will last forever—faith, hope, and love—and the greatest of these is love.

I Corinthians 13:4-7,13 NLT

ABOUT THE AUTHOR

Pamela Adams is a businesswoman, author, speaker, artist, and single mother of three refusing to be anything less than what God has called her to be. She knows that her past does not define nor limit what her future holds. She is an encourager and worshipper of Jesus Christ. Adams attends God's Holy Tabernacle for All People Outreach Ministries of Twin City, Georgia. There she is a youth teacher and worship leader. She believes in being positive despite what it "looks like". She enjoys uplifting others, listening to music, beach therapy, and taking naps. Adams is the founder and CEO of Discovering Life's Possibilities, LLC and currently serves as an accountant at East Georgia State College.

To contact the author for speaking engagements or other inquiries, please send emails to info@discoveringlifespossibilities.com.

*Bulk orders must be paid for in advance. Once payment has been received in the bank, books will be shipped within 14 business days.

Are you seeking to tell your story, but don't know where to start?

Have you already written your book, but have not taken the next steps to get it published?

Let DLP Publishing help you!!!

Made in the USA
Columbia, SC
25 February 2019